# This or That

# Questions
## About
## Animals and Plants

# You Decide!

by Kathryn Clay

CAPSTONE PRESS
a capstone imprint

Capstone Captivate is published by Capstone Press, an imprint of Capstone.
1710 Roe Crest Drive
North Mankato, Minnesota 56003
www.capstonepub.com

**Library of Congress Cataloging-in-Publication Data is available on the Library of Congress website.**
ISBN: 978-1-4966-9567-3 (library binding)
ISBN: 978-1-4966-9695-3 (paperback)
ISBN: 978-1-9771-5510-8 (eBook PDF)

Summary: Presents intriguing questions and information related to animals and plants and prompts readers to pick one choice or the other.

**Image Credits**
Shutterstock: Abdul Gapur Dayak, 15, Chr. Offenberg, 3, Damsea, 7, Darren Kurnia, 24, David T Clarke, 20, GoodStudio, design element, imacoconut, 25, Jeff Holcombe, 17, Kwangmoozaa, 22, LouisLotterPhotography, 10, marilyn barbone, 12, Mark_Kostich, 11, mavo, 27, max amorntap, 4–5, Mirko Graul, 23, MIROFOSS, 19, MR.AUKID PHUMSIRICHAT, design element, Nate Hovee, 8, Neel Adsul, cover bottom left, Niney Azman, 14, nutsiam, 21, Ondrej Prosicky, cover top left, ParthaKar49, 13, Patila, 16, Pixel-Shot, 26, Rob Byron, 9, Roop_Dey, 29, Suhanova Kseniya, 28, Vova Shevchuk, 6, William Cushman, 18, Yuriy Kulik, cover bottom right

**Editorial Credits**
Editors: Michelle Parkin and Carrie Sheely; Designer: Sarah Bennett; Media Researcher: Tracy Cummins; Production Specialist: Spencer Rosio

All internet sites appearing in back matter were available and accurate when this book was sent to press.

Words in **bold** are in the glossary.

# The Wide World of Animals and Plants

Take a look outside. Life is all around you! Scientists estimate that 8.7 million animal **species** live on Earth. That number includes 6.5 million land animals and 2.2 million ocean animals. There are about 400,000 plant species. These numbers keep growing as scientists discover new plants and animals.

Animals and plants all have features that make them unique. Many are amazing. Some lizards can change color. Some trees grow more than 300 feet (91 meters) tall. But other things aren't so pleasant. Dung beetles eat animal poop. Some plants smell terrible. Welcome to the diverse—and sometimes disgusting—world of animals and plants!

# How to Use This Book

This book is full of questions that will keep you thinking about different plants and animals. Following each question are details to help you make a decision. Pick one choice or the other. There are no wrong answers. For some questions, the answer might seem easy. For others, you will need to think carefully.

Once you've decided, check with your friends and family. Would they make the same choice? Share with them why you made the choice that you did. Then listen to their reasons for each choice. It might spark a fun debate.

Are you ready? Turn the page to pick this or that!

✓ have one stinger

✓ very painful

✓ rarely deadly

About 1,500 species of scorpions live around the world. A scorpion has a long tail with a stinger at the end. Each year, people report about 1.2 million scorpion stings. These stings can cause intense pain, numbness, tingling, and swelling. Severe stings can lead to breathing difficulties, muscle twitching, drooling, and vomiting. But scorpion stings are rarely deadly. Only 30 to 40 kinds produce enough **venom** to kill a person.

- ✓ have thousands of stingers
- ✓ causes rashes and blisters
- ✓ stings from some species can cause death

Jellyfish are known for their painful stings. They inject venom from thousands of barbed stingers. Stings can leave painful rashes and cause a burning or itchy feeling. Box jellyfish stings are some of the worst. Their stings can cause stomach pain, headaches, breathing difficulties, and even heart problems. Without fast medical treatment, they can lead to death.

- ✔ long spines
- ✔ not poisonous
- ✔ can cause serious infections

Imagine going on a desert hike and bumping into something sharp. Ouch! Many cactuses are covered in long spines. Cactus spines aren't poisonous. But some are covered in **bacteria** and **fungi**. The spines can cause serious skin infections if left in your skin for too long.

✓ causes allergic reaction

✓ causes itchy rash

✓ can cause oozing blisters

Poison ivy leaves, stems, and roots are covered in a sticky oil. Most people are **allergic** to it. Touching poison ivy causes an itchy rash that can last for weeks. Scratching itchy skin can cause it to crack and become infected. Your skin can swell with oozing blisters.

# This ▶ be covered with feathers

- ✓ might not fly
- ✓ so much cleaning
- ✓ limited ability to grasp and hold objects

You may want feathers like a bird. But even with feathers, there's no guarantee you could fly. Just look at ostriches and penguins. They have feathers, but they can't fly. Feathers also require lots of cleaning. Birds spend much of their time **preening** to remove rocks, sand, and bugs. And you can forget about playing video games. You wouldn't be able to press buttons or hold remotes if your hands were covered in feathers.

- ✓ regular shedding of skin
- ✓ can't sweat
- ✓ good protection

How does flaky skin sound? Reptiles have **scales**, and they shed their skin as they grow. Scales are waterproof. This could be helpful in rain. But you wouldn't be able to sweat. Without sweat, you wouldn't be able to control your body temperature. Scales would provide some protection from injuries while climbing or during other activities.

✓ live more than 1,000 years

✓ higher chance of being struck by lightning

✓ can get diseases

Oak trees can live more than 1,000 years. They produce up to 10 million acorns in a lifetime. At 60 to 100 feet (18 to 30 m) tall, oak trees are more likely to be struck by lightning than shorter trees. They are also commonly affected by diseases that can damage their leaves and roots. Beetles can also tunnel into the bark and lay eggs.

# That? be a giant water lily

- ✓ grow up to 9 feet (3 m) across
- ✓ flowers have sweet smell
- ✓ attract beetles

Giant water lilies can grow up to 9 feet (2.7 m) across and hold more than 100 pounds (45 kilograms). Animals sometimes walk or sit on them. Giant water lilies live in shallow parts of the Amazon River in South America. Their flowers smell like butterscotch and pineapple. This might be nice—until the beetles come! The sweet smell attracts beetles that **pollinate** the plants. Giant water lilies die out but grow back each growing season.

13

✓ longer than a ruler

✓ 300 to 400 tiny legs

✓ stinky when scared

Giant African millipedes live in African
**rain forests**. Most millipedes are 1 to 2 inches
(2.5 to 5 centimeters) long. But the giant version
can grow up to 15 inches (38 cm) long. That's
longer than a ruler! Now imagine 300 to 400 tiny
legs crawling across your skin. When scared, giant
millipedes curl into a ball. They might release a stinky
liquid that can irritate your eyes and skin.

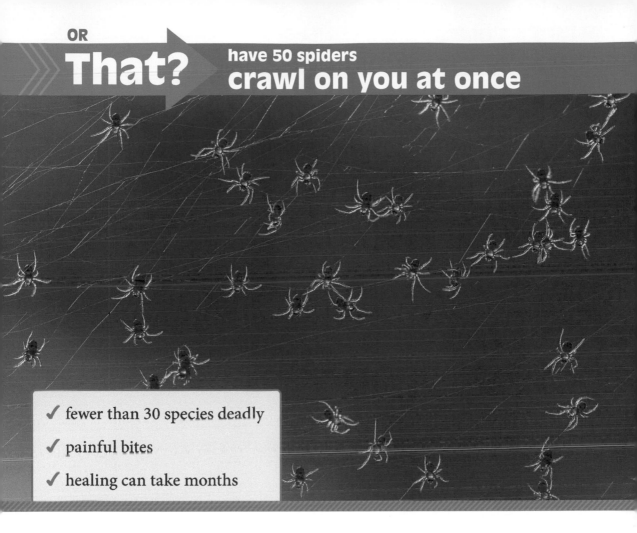

✓ fewer than 30 species deadly

✓ painful bites

✓ healing can take months

Some people believe a crawling spider brings good luck. But few people would feel lucky with 50 spiders on them! Most spiders are harmless. Of the more than 43,000 species, fewer than 30 are deadly to humans. But spider bites can be painful. Full healing from some bites can take months.

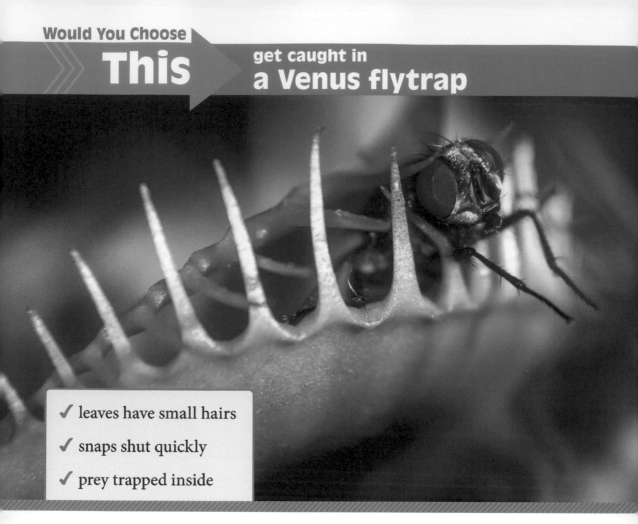

✓ leaves have small hairs

✓ snaps shut quickly

✓ prey trapped inside

What makes Venus flytraps unique? They eat meat! Thin extensions surround their leaves. The plant keeps its leaves open. Tiny hairs cover the leaves. Insects or small frogs touch the hairs on a leaf. Snap! The leaf closes in less than a second! The leaf seals up to keep the **prey** locked inside. Dinner is served!

✓ cup-like leaves

✓ nectar causes sleepiness

✓ prey trapped inside

Pitcher plants are some of the largest meat-eating plants. Long, cup-like leaves stick out from thick stems. The cups are lined with a sweet **nectar** that attracts insects and small rodents. The animals drink the nectar, which makes them sleepy. They fall into the cup with no way to get out. The prey dies, and the plant digests its meal.

✓ causes drooling

✓ causes digestive problems

✓ can be deadly

Mountain death camas plants have white flowers and small bulbs that look like onions. They grow mostly in western parts of the United States. Eating death camas can cause drooling, vomiting, and diarrhea. A single bulb from a mountain death camas can sicken animals and humans. Eating too many can be deadly. Some early U.S. settlers died when they mistook this plant for a wild onion.

# That? eat a snakeroot plant

- ✓ causes stomach pain
- ✓ recovery can be slow
- ✓ can be deadly

Snakeroot plants grow in eastern Canada and the United States. While the roots are safe, the leaves and stems are highly poisonous. Eating them can cause stomach pain, trembling, weakness, and vomiting. Recovery can take weeks. In severe cases, the poison can cause death. People sometimes get poisoned after drinking milk from cows that have eaten the plants.

- ✓ molts to grow
- ✓ has to continually look for new shells
- ✓ no protection while without a shell

A shell protects a hermit crab's soft belly from **predators** and keeps it from drying out. To grow, hermit crabs **molt**. Then the crabs need bigger shells. Hermit crabs use many shells throughout their lives. They often find shells that snails have left behind. Until it finds a new shell, a hermit crab has no protection. Hermit crabs also fight over shells. These fights can cause injuries.

✓ provides good protection

✓ can flip over and get stuck

✓ can get shell rot

Hard plates called **scutes** make up a turtle's shell. The shell provides safety and a home that's always available. But it can't protect a turtle from everything. There's always the risk of flipping over and getting stuck. Shell rot happens when bacteria or fungi get stuck in the shell. This can lead to an infection that can damage the turtle's **organs**. If the shell becomes damaged, the turtle can't replace its shell.

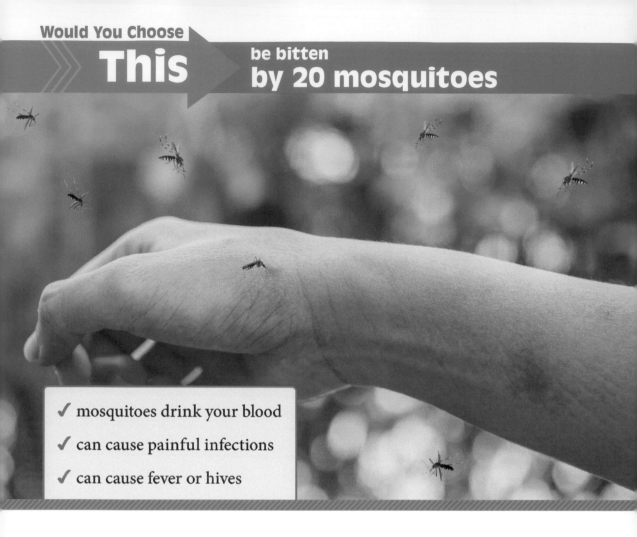

✔ mosquitoes drink your blood

✔ can cause painful infections

✔ can cause fever or hives

Female mosquitoes bite to drink your blood to make babies. Their saliva goes into your skin and keeps your blood from clotting. This keeps blood flowing. Your body makes a chemical to fight the saliva, which results in a small, itchy bump. Scratching too hard can break the skin and cause painful infections. For some people, mosquito bites can cause a fever or hives.

✓ barbed stinger stays in skin

✓ painful venom

✓ can cause death for people with allergies

When a honeybee stings you, its stinger stays in your skin. It can release venom for up to one minute. A sting causes sharp pain and swelling. Many other kinds of bees can sting more than once. People with severe allergies to bee venom may have trouble breathing. Without a special shot of medicine, they can die.

✓ smells like rotten meat

✓ smell attracts beetles and flies

✓ blooms for a short time

Huge corpse flowers are found in the rain forests of Indonesia. Some grow more than 10 feet (3 m) tall. Most grow seven to 10 years before blooming. That might be a good thing. Their flowers smell like rotten meat. The horrible smell attracts beetles and flies. Thankfully, corpse flowers bloom for no longer than about two days.

be stuck in a room with
**a female ginkgo tree**

- ✔ attractive trees
- ✔ rotting fruits smell like vomit
- ✔ touching fruit can cause itchy rashes

Ginkgo trees have been around more than 200 million years. The tall trees have fan-shaped leaves that turn a golden color in fall. But female ginkgoes have a stinky surprise. After their fruits fall from the branches, they rot and smell like vomit. If the smell doesn't keep you away, touching the fruit can give you itchy rashes.

✓ can know what animals need

✓ can't control what you hear

✓ might hear about exciting adventures

Talking with an animal would help you be sure of what it wants or needs. It might be fun to have a deep conversation with a goldfish or chat with your cat. Animals might be able to share interesting information with you about their adventures. Maybe your cat or dog would tell you about a hunting trip. But you can't control what an animal might say. What if you didn't like what a pet said? It could hurt the relationship with your pet.

## OR
## That?  talk with plants

✓ can know what plants need

✓ no more quiet walks in the woods

✓ screaming lawns

If you could talk with plants, you would know how to care for them. But the world would be a much noisier place. Your ears might be blasted by flowers, trees, and grass as you take a walk in the woods. With less active lives, plants might have less exciting experiences to talk about than animals. But plants might have a lot to say about picking flowers or mowing your lawn!

- ✓ similar to riding a horse
- ✓ good for traveling over rough land
- ✓ can be stubborn

People around the world use donkeys for transportation. Donkeys are strong, smart, and calm. They can handle traveling on rough, rocky land. You would need to make regular stops for water and food. Riding donkeys is similar to riding horses. But donkeys can be stubborn and refuse to move. If you plan to ride a donkey to school, you'd better set your alarm extra early!

✓ strong

✓ good for desert travel

✓ might cause sore leg muscles

In desert areas, people use camels for transportation. They can handle hot desert weather better than donkeys. You would likely need to make fewer stops when traveling by camel. As long as they have food, camels can go for months without water. Like donkeys, camels are strong. But before hopping on a camel, you may want to stretch a bit. Camels sway back and forth as they walk. Many people report sore leg muscles after a long ride.

# Lightning Round
## Would you choose to . . .

→ stun prey with an electric charge like an electric eel **or** spit silk and venom to trap prey like a spitting spider?

→ live on an apple orchard **or** a dairy farm?

→ harvest pungent durian fruit **or** heavy jackfruits?

→ eat a whole onion **or** a whole lemon?

→ have an elephant-sized cat **or** a cat-sized elephant?

→ be bitten by a giant desert centipede **or** a bullet ant?

→ have a tail that can't grab things **or** wings that can't fly?

→ be raised by a herd of elephants **or** a pod of dolphins?